RAPTURE

RAPTURE
WILL YOU BE TAKEN?

BY: DUANE FLANAGAN

XULON PRESS

Xulon Press
2301 Lucien Way #415
Maitland, FL 32751
407.339.4217
www.xulonpress.com

Scripture quotations taken from the King James Version (KJV) – *public domain.*

All word definitions are taken from *Strong's Concordance.*

Printed in the United States of America.

ISBN-13: 978-1-54565-655-6

Contents

Introduction

T he purpose of this book is to open the Bible and allow the truth that is written to open our minds and expand our thinking. Every Christian should be able to gain valuable insights as the written Word of God is read and understood.

There are some that will read this book and be amazed at the insight presented. There are others that will scoff at it and attempt to belittle its contents.

In most cases, our minds are either open or closed concerning biblical topics. These conditions stem directly from what we have been taught. These very contrasts should challenge us to keep an open mind and look at this material objectively.

This book is obviously not an exhaustive resource, and it was not designed for that purpose. Its objective is to be a short, eye opening resource which sparks further investigation from us.

Many Christians start reading a 100-200-page book with the best intentions. However, thirty to fifty pages later, it is placed on our bookshelves and joins the other partially-read books. This book can be read in a short period of time and hopefully sheds light on this supernatural topic.

I pray this little book will be a blessing to you and enrich your Christian walk.

Duane Flanagan

Chapter One

The Word *Rapture*

In present day Christianity, the word *rapture* is a common-ly-used term. It symbolizes a belief by many Christians of an approaching event by which our Lord Jesus will return. At the point of this return, He will receive dead and living Christians unto Himself. This idea brings hope to those who believe in such an event and irritation to those that doubt its validity. The very thought of such a massive supernatural event boggles the mind, even for those who believe it will happen.

There are some churches and Christian groups that have a problem using the word *rapture* without scoffing. A common concern is the word *rapture* is found nowhere in the Bible. How can a word that is not even used in Scripture generate so much belief and disbelief at the same time? How can a Christian article or book be credible and scripturally accurate using terminology the Bible doesn't use? Where did the word *rapture* come from? These are all legitimate questions that deserve explanations.

"The English word *rapture* comes from the Latin word *rapturo*, which is a translation of the Greek verb *aJrpavzw*, or, *harpazo*."[1]

---

[1] Thayer and Smith. "Greek Lexicon entry for Harpazo," "The KJV New Testament Greek Lexi con."

Harpazo (har-pad'-zo) means to be "caught up," and is found in the apostle Paul's first letter to the Christians at Thessalonica.

> *Then we who are alive and remain shall be caught*
> *up [harpazo, rapturo] together with them in the*
> *clouds, to meet the Lord in the air; and so shall we*
> *ever be with the Lord.*
>
> 1 Thessalonians 4:17

When Paul wrote this letter to the Thessalonian believers, he used the Greek language, which was the language of his day. Actually, the entire New Testament was written in Greek by the various authors whose writings were compiled to provide the content of it.

When the Vulgate, which is the Latin translation of Scripture, was translated from the original Greek language, the word *rapturo* was used in verse 17 as "caught up" (*harpazo*). Because Latin has influenced about a third of the English language, the word *rapturo* became *rapture*. The word *rapture* is used more as a term for a coming event versus a direct translation of one.

The direct translation from the Greek verb *harpazo* into the English is: "to catch, steal, carry off, and caught up." [2]

For those who have a problem using the word *rapture,* let's say this: even though the word itself is not used in the Bible, its meaning is clearly established. We should take notice of additional scriptures where *harpazo* is used:

> *[2]I knew a man in Christ above fourteen years ago*
> *(whether in the body, I cannot tell; or whether out*
> *of the body, I cannot tell: God knoweth) such an*
> *one "caught up" (harpazo) to the third heaven. [3]*
> *And I knew such a man (whether in the body, or*

---

[2] Strong's Concordance

out of the body, I cannot tell: God knoweth). *⁴How*
he was "caught up" (harpazo) into paradise and
heard unspeakable words, which it is not lawful for
a man to utter.

2 Corinthians 12:2-4

Some may say Paul was caught up spiritually and not physically. Either way, he was "caught up" (*harpazo, rapturo*) to the
third heaven (paradise):

First heaven = clouds
Second heaven = stars
Third heaven = paradise

What we should notice is how Paul uses the same verb *harpazo*
(*rapturo, caught up*) in his letter to the Corinthian believers when
describing an event that has happened to him. It should be safe to
assume that his usage of the verb *harpazo* in an event he did experience is just as real as his usage of *harpazo* to the Thessalonian
Christian of a future event.

The apostle Luke also uses *harpazo* when recording the Acts
of the Apostles:

³⁹And when they were come up out of the water, the
Spirit of the Lord "caught away" (harpazo) Phillip,
that the eunuch saw him no more; and he went on
his way rejoicing. ⁴⁰But Phillip was found at Azotus;
and passing through, he preached in all the cities
till he came to Caesarea.

Acts 8:39-40

The Bible doesn't record the level to which Phillip was "caught
away" (*harpazo, rapturo*) before he was found at Azotus, which is
about thirty miles from where he baptized the eunuch. It may be

3

safe to assume that Phillip was "caught away" in the first heaven (clouds); which is the same place the dead and living Christians will be meeting the Lord Jesus upon his return.

Let us look at one more example of the verb *harpazo* being used in John's description of the revelation he received from the Lord Jesus, on the Isle of Patmos.

> *And she brought forth a male child, who was to rule*
> *all nations with a rod of iron; and her child was*
> *"caught up" (harpazo) unto God, and to his throne.*
>
> Revelation 12:5

This is a clear description of the Lord Jesus as he ascended into heaven that is recorded in Acts 1:9.

Hopefully the scriptures we have looked at give a clear understanding of the word *rapture*. Whether one decides to use the Greek verb *harpazo*, or the Latin verb *rapturo*, or even the English verb *caught up*, they all have the same meaning. Because of this, we will use the word *rapture* in this book as a point of contact and identification.

Now let's look at what the word *rapture* represents: a change in location for one group of people and no location change for another group of individuals.

> ⁴⁰*Then shall two be in the field; the one shall be*
> *taken (paralembano) and the other left (aphiemi).*
> ⁴¹*Two women shall be grinding at the mill; the one*
> *shall be taken (paralembano) and the other left*
> *(aphiemi).*
>
> Matthew 24:40-41

In both of these verses, our Lord Jesus uses two Greek verbs: *paralembano*, which means "to take with," "take charge of," and then also "to receive." The second verb is *aphiemi*, meaning "to leave" or "to abandon."[3]

Christ clearly describes a location change for one and not the other by using the words "taken" and "left" in these verses.

> *And while they went to buy, the bridegroom came,*
> *and they that were ready went in with him to the*
> *marriage; and the door was shut.*
>
> Matthew 25:10

In this parable, Christ uses the Greek verb *eisershonmai*, meaning "to go in, went into, enter in through." He is clearly describing a change of location for the ones who were ready. The doorway to this new location is also shut after those who are ready enter in. Those who were not ready are not allowed access through this closed doorway. This description which Christ uses clearly teaches that this new location for those who are ready is not an earthly location.

Up to this point, we have looked at the meaning of the word *rapture* and also what it represents. A study of this supernatural event would not be complete without addressing the predictions of "when" it will take place. There is a vast supply of material that discusses and supports the three most popular positions about a coming rapture:

1. Pre-tribulation: before the Great Tribulation
2. Mid-tribulation: three-and-a-half years into the Great Tribulation
3. Post-tribulation: at the end of the Great Tribulation

---

[3] Strong's Concordance

The Great Tribulation is a seven-year period described in the Bible as an earth-shattering time unlike any other that has ever occurred on our planet. Christ describes it as follows:

> *For then shall be great tribulation, such as was not since the beginning of the world to this time, no, nor shall ever be.*
>
> Matthew 24:21

The purpose of this book is not to discuss the timing of the rapture or attempt to predict when it will take place. This book will concentrate on the more personal issues of who will be taken and why, and also who will be left behind and why.

Personal participation, or lack of it, would seem to be a more relevant issue to each one of us. Realistically speaking, as long as we are ready, the timing of the rapture is of lesser importance. Let's leave the precise timing of the rapture to the Bible scholars and, ultimately, to God the Father himself.

Many Christian churches teach that when Christ returns, all converted (born-again) believers will be taken in an event referred to as the rapture. There are a number of books and movies that point out to us that there are three general people groups on earth:

1. Committed Christians serving God.
2. People who believe they are Christians because they believe in God, but really aren't serving God.
3. The unsaved.

When group #1, committed Christians, are taken in the rapture, group #2, people who believe they are Christians, will realize that their life has not involved committed service to God. They will realize the error of their ways after being left behind and become wonderfully devoted Christians, helping others to see the light in a time of intense tribulation on earth. We will search the Scriptures and investigate the accuracy of these beliefs.

Perhaps we should end this chapter by exposing a "myth" that seems to be gaining momentum in some areas of Christianity. Let's take another look at 1 Thessalonians 4:17:

> *Then we who are alive and remain shall be caught*
> *up together with them in the clouds, to meet the Lord*
> *in the air and so shall we ever be with the Lord.*

It has been supposed by some teachers the word "air" in verse 17 is talking about the air that we breathe. They use that point to support their beliefs that this so-called rapture is not a removal of Christians, but rather a gathering together of Christians in the air that we breathe on the earth. Therefore, 1 Thessalonians 4:17 actually describes the second coming of Christ, which will begin His thousand-year reign on earth, commonly known as the "Millennium Reign."

If you know anything about mountain climbing, breathable air exists up to approximately 18,000 feet. That elevation is called the "vertical limit." The air above 18,000 feet does not contain enough oxygen to support life for extended periods of time. Therefore, anywhere between ground level and 18,000 feet, breathable air exists. Why concentrate on the bottom six feet of breathable air and build a doctrine based on that?

Let's instead use the "breathable air" truth and incorporate it into the other information the Bible gives us!

In 1 Thessalonians 4:17 Paul describes being "caught up," indicating a rise in elevation. If he were describing the bottom six feet of breathable air, we would be caught over, not up. Another truth that should grab our attention is being caught up in the "clouds." Normal cloud elevation is anywhere between 6,500 feet and 45,000 feet. [4]

---

[4] "Types of Clouds and How They Form," Cloud Information and Types, National Geographic, 9 Apr. 2017.

So let us recap using all the information in 1 Thessalonians 4:16-17. The dead in Christ and the alive in Christ will be caught up in the air that we breathe, where clouds normally exist, to meet the Lord. Considering that this gathering is going to involve a large volume of people, one would have to agree that a little height in elevation might be needed: somewhere between 6,500 feet and 18,000 feet, where clouds normally exist and breathable air also exists—also, where there is enough room for millions upon millions of Christians to assemble.

Here's a thought: how about we let the Bible expand our thinking, rather than trying to get the Bible to match what we think?

Chapter Two

Rapturing

A **Consistent Biblical Theme**

I n the previous chapter, we looked at scriptures that clearly define a future catching away of dead and living Christians. Let's back up to Genesis and begin looking at individuals that have already been caught away (raptured).

The first recorded instance of a supernatural catching away in Scripture is Enoch. He was the seventh generation from Adam, and the Bible clearly documents in the Old and New Testaments that Enoch was physically removed from the earth, without experiencing natural death. God chose to seize and transport him from the earth, to the realm where God Himself resides. It could be said that he was *raptured*. First mention of this is in Genesis 5:22-24, and then Hebrews 11:5:

> ²²*And Enoch walked with God after he begot Methuselah three hundred years and begot sons and daughters. ²³And all the days of Enoch were three hundred sixty and five years. ²⁴And Enoch walked with God, and he was not; for God took him.*
>
> Genesis 5:22-24

By faith Enoch was translated that he should not see death and was not found because God had translated him; for before his translation he had this testimony, that he pleased God.

Hebrews 11:5

We should not have a hard time believing that as creator, God reserves the right to rapture individuals or groups at His own will. He is all-powerful, all-knowing, and everywhere at once. Rapturing an individual person or a group of people is but a small thing for the King of the Universe!

NOAH

There is a teaching in the Christian ranks that says Noah was not raptured because he did not leave the earth. He remained, and the wicked were taken away. Therefore, Noah's experience couldn't be considered a rapture experience because there was no change in location for him or his family. Let's look at what the Bible has recorded about the Great Flood.

[17] And the flood was forty days upon the earth; and the waters increased and bore up the ark, and it was lifted up above the earth. [18]And the waters prevailed, and were increased greatly upon the earth; and the ark went upon the face of the waters. [19]And the waters prevailed exceedingly upon the earth; and all the high hills, that were under the whole heaven, were covered. [20]Fifteen cubits upward did the waters prevail; and the mountains were covered.

Genesis 7:17-20

Notice verse 17, which clearly describes the Ark as being lifted up above the earth. Verses 19 and 20 say that all the high hills and mountains were covered. Obviously, the entirety of the planet was covered with water, and no dry ground was to be found. Even the tallest mountains were under water. Therefore, if the Ark was floating above the tallest mountains, it clearly stands to reason that the inhabitants of the Ark were no longer on the earth. They were above it.

The Ark and its inhabitants were removed (raptured) from the earth to a safe place above the earth. The rest of creation remained in an unsafe place on earth and experienced tribulation. After the tribulation, which came in the form of a flood, ended, Noah and his family returned to earth.

The Book of Revelation gives us an account of the church's removal from earth, which is known in modern terminology as "the rapture." When this removal (rapture) occurs, the ones left behind experience great tribulation. After this seven-year period ends, the Lord Jesus returns to earth with His family (the church) to set up His thousand-year, "Millennial Reign." This would certainly seem to be the reason the Lord Jesus uses Noah's experience in Matthew 24 when describing the rapture.

What an amazing picture the Lord Jesus paints for us using Old Testament scriptures and the story of Noah!

ELIJAH

Mentioned in Old Testament scripture, God used the prophet Elijah in mighty ways throughout his earthly ministry. Elijah reappears in the New Testament with Moses, at the transfiguration of Christ.

Just like Enoch, Elijah was bodily removed (raptured) to heaven without experiencing natural death. The difference between the two is that Enoch's removal is only described as a translation, and there were no eyewitnesses. Contrarily, Elijah's servant Elisha, who was anointed after his removal from earth, witnessed Elijah's experience. God used a natural phenomenon (whirlwind or tornado) to remove Elijah.

> *And it came to pass, as they still went on, and talked, that, behold, there appeared a chariot of fire, and horses of fire, and separated them, and Elijah went up by a whirlwind into heaven.*
>
> 2 Kings 2:11

JESUS CHRIST

All professing believers know the story of how Jesus of Nazareth was crucified for the sins of all mankind. This single act of substitution also restored the original relationship between God the Father and His creation.

Christ hung on the cross for six hours and died with the words, "It is finished." The number six represents mankind because the first man, Adam, was created on the sixth and final day of creation. This numerical symbolism—Christ's dying in the sixth hour and the symbolism of the number six itself—demonstrates that Jesus was the sinless substitute for all of mankind.

Jesus was placed in a tomb where His body remained for three days and three nights (72 hours), just like the prophet Jonah.

> *For as Jonah was three days and three nights in the belly of the great fish, so shall the son of man be three days and three nights in the heart of the earth.*
>
> Matthew 12:40

After this 72-hour period was fulfilled, the Lord Jesus rose from the dead. He walked on earth for forty days being seen by His disciples and many others. At the end of this forty-day period, the Lord Jesus ascended (raptured) into heaven out of a crowd of many witnesses, as they watched him go.

> *[50]And he led them out as far as to Bethany, and he lifted up his hands, and blessed them. [51]And it came to pass, while he blessed them, he was parted from them, and carried "up" into heaven.*
>
> Luke 24:50-51

> *[9]And when he had spoken these things, while they beheld, he was "taken up," and a cloud received him out of their sight. [10]And while they looked up steadfastly, toward heaven as he "went up," behold, two men stood by them in white apparel.*
>
> Acts 1:9-10

PAUL THE APOSTLE

Paul began as Saul of Tarshish, persecutor of believers in Christ. He was constantly breathing out threats and slaughter against believers of a resurrected Christ. Equipped with arrest papers from the Sanhedrin, Saul was rounding up Christians to be placed on trial before the religious leaders of the day. Saul consented to and witnessed the stoning of Steven after his trial and testimony. On the road to Damascus, Saul fell to the ground by a light that shone from heaven, and the Lord spoke to him.

> *[3]And as he journeyed, he came near Damascus, and suddenly there shined round about him a light from heaven. [4]And he fell to the earth, and heard a voice saying unto him, Saul, Saul why persecutes thou me? [7]And the men who journeyed with him stood speechless, hearing a voice, but seeing no man.*
>
> Acts 9:3-4,7

Some say that Saul was knocked off his donkey. No donkeys are listed as being present. The Bible does say that Saul fell to the

13

ground and those with him stood and witnessed this event. More than likely, what happened was: they were all walking down the road nearing Damascus with Saul in the lead. The light shone from heaven, and Saul fell to the ground. The others with him stopped walking, stood still, and witnessed this supernatural encounter.

> *[2] I knew a man in Christ above fourteen years ago (whether in the body, I cannot tell; or whether out of the body, I cannot tell; God knoweth) – such an one "caught up" to the third heaven. [3] And I knew such a man (whether in the body, or out of the body, I cannot tell; God knoweth). [4] How he was "caught up" into paradise, and heard unspeakable words, which is not lawful for a man to utter.*
>
> 2 Corinthians 12:2-4

In verse 2 and verse 4, Paul talks about being "caught up" (raptured) to the third heaven, or paradise. Paul is not sure if he was physically caught up or spiritually caught up. Either way, it seems noteworthy to include this in a chapter containing raptured individuals or groups.

PHILLIP and the Ethiopian Eunuch

Because Phillip's rapture was covered in chapter one, we will not repeat it. Up to this point, the raptures that have been recorded in the Bible have already happened and involve individuals only. The next mentioned raptures are future events and have not yet occurred.

The TWO WITNESSES of Revelation

> *[11] And after three days and a half the spirit of life from God entered into them, and they stood upon their*

14

> *feet, and great fear fell upon them who saw them.*
> *[12]And they heard a great voice from heaven saying*
> *unto them, Come up here. And they "ascended up"*
> *to heaven in a cloud, and their enemies beheld them.*
> Revelation 11:11-12

These two prophets mentioned are sent to prophesy on earth during the last three-and-a-half years of the Great Tribulation. Notice that after their death and resurrection, they "ascend up" to heaven in a cloud as their enemies witness this supernatural event. These two unique prophets exit the earth in a very similar fashion as did the Lord Jesus.

The BODY OF CHRIST (both past and present)

> *[31]And he shall send his angels with a great sound of*
> *a trumpet, and they shall gather together his elect*
> *from the four winds, from one end of heaven to the*
> *other. [40]Then shall two be in the field; the one shall*
> *be taken, and the other left. [41]Two women shall be*
> *grinding at the mill; the one shall be taken, and the*
> *other left.*
> Matthew 24:31, 40, 41

The Lord Jesus clearly describes a worldwide gathering of His elect in verse 31. In verses 40 and 41, He further breaks it down for us to an individual experience. He points out in vivid detail that a removal (rapturing) of His elect and a leaving behind of non-elect is for certain. His usage of the words "taken and left" should clearly point out that truth to us.

> *[16]For the Lord himself shall descend from heaven*
> *with a shout, with the voice of the archangel, and*
> *with the trump of God; and the dead in Christ shall*

rise first. [17]Then we who are alive and remain shall be caught up together with them in the clouds, to meet the Lord in the air; and so shall we ever be with the Lord.

1 Thessalonians 4:16-17

In his letter to the Thessalonian Christians, Paul also gives us a detailed look at the entire rapture sequence.

1. The Lord Jesus descends from heaven with a shout
2. The voice of the archangel announcing the Lord
3. The trumpet of God sounding
4. The dead in Christ rising (resurrecting)
5. We who are alive being "caught up" (raptured)

This chapter should clearly point out to us that catching away (rapturing) is a consistent Biblical occurrence. Why should the future catching away (rapturing) of dead and living Christians be any different? Why should we have such a hard time believing something that has so many scriptural examples? If we don't believe in a literal rapture, it is because we don't want to believe it.

Let us end with this cliché: Many Christians do not let the Bible get in the way of what they want to believe.

Chapter Three

In the Twinkling of an Eye

This is a common expression that most people (Christians and non-believers) have a fair understanding of. It is a second in time, or a portion of a second. It passes so fast that it is almost unmeasurable.

Many Christian churches teach that when the Lord Jesus returns to rapture the church (His body), all the Christians will be caught away so fast that no one will see it or know what happened to them. The naked human eye will not be able to see or record this supernatural event.

Just imagine, for a moment, what this implicates.

Christian pilots will disappear, and their planes will be left to fly themselves, ultimately to crash. Cars, trains, and buses also will crash as Christian drivers are extracted from earth in the twinkling of an eye. Thousands—maybe millions of people—will be left behind and die as a result of unattended moving vehicles crashing. Chaos and confusion will follow as the people who are left behind will have no idea what happened to the people that will be taken.

Is this really what the Bible teaches? Or is this simply a religious concept that takes a couple of scriptures and builds a doctrine out of them, while other scriptures are ignored? Let us explore this further and see what Scripture says.

> *For yourselves know perfectly that the day of the Lord so cometh as a thief in the night.*
>
> 1 Thessalonians 5:2

> *[51]Behold, I show you a mystery: we shall not all sleep, but we shall all be changed. [52]In a moment, in the twinkling of an eye, at the last trump; for the trumpet shall sound, and the dead shall be raised incorruptible, and we shall be changed.*
>
> 1 Corinthians 15:51-52

Most rapture teachers would say these accounts are evidence enough to support the claim of a "twinkling of an eye," that these two scriptural references clearly teach an immediate removal of dead and living Christians from the earth.

Let us think about what it says for a moment. When a thief comes to rob you, does he do so in the twinkling of an eye? Does he just drive by and immediately extract your material possessions? No, he has to sneak in and carry them out. It is a process, not an instant result.

"As a thief in the night" is describing the timing of the event (because we do not know when it will happen), not the actual process. If we had known when the thief was coming, we would have been sure to be ready for him. If we had known when the Lord Jesus would return, we would be sure to be ready for Him.

Some teachings suggest that the phrase in verse 52, "in the twinkling of an eye," clearly shows how fast the rapture will take place. It does say that in the twinkling of an eye we shall be changed (transfigured). The verse doesn't say that in the twinkling of an eye we shall all disappear.

This is a clear example of building a doctrine based on a couple of scriptural references. It is easy to take them out of context when doing that. Let's add some additional verses to open our eyes and put the entire rapture process into context.

> *[42]Watch, therefore, for ye know not what "hour" your Lord doth come. [44]Therefore be ye also ready; for in such an "hour" as ye think not the son of man cometh. [50]The lord of that servant shall come in a day when he looketh not for him, and in an "hour" that he is not aware of."*
>
> Matthew 24:42, 44, 50

Perhaps we should notice in these verses by Christ that three times He uses the word *hour*. It's interesting to note that He does not use the term "split-second" when describing His return.

> *[6]And at midnight there was a cry made, Behold, the bridegroom cometh; go yet out to meet him. [7]Then all those virgins arose and trimmed their lamps. [8]And the foolish said unto the wise, Give us your oil; for our lamps have gone out. [9]But the wise answered, saying Not so, lest there be not enough for us and you; but go rather to them that sell, and buy for yourselves. [10]And while they went to buy, the bridegroom came, and they that were ready went in with him to the marriage; and the door was shut.*
>
> Matthew 25:6-10

A couple of things in these verses should stand out to us. All ten virgins (who represent Christians) heard the cry that was made. They all rose and trimmed their lamps—which is a process; not a split-second occurrence. The foolish had time to say to the wise, "Give us some of your oil." The wise had time to answer and give

19

them some advice. The foolish also had time to go out and attempt to fix the issue of oil before the wise were taken. These verses clearly teach a rapture *process*, not a split-second disappearance.

At this point, let us stop for a moment and address a concern that some may have. Some may say that you can't take a parable like Matthew 25, the Parable of the Ten Virgins, literally. At the beginning of the previous chapter, Matthew 24, Jesus answers some questions His disciples ask Him concerning the end of the age and His return. The entire chapter is devoted to many aspects of His return, such as signs and conditions on earth. He also points out the removal of some and the leaving behind of others.

Jesus continues on in Matthew 25, in parable form, to share additional insights about why some will be taken and why some will be left. Remember that Matthew 25 is still part of the same answer that began in Matthew 24.

The Lord Jesus also knew that the disciples would ask why some would be taken and others would be left, as He said in Matthew 24:40-41. So Jesus' answer comes in Matthew 25, in parable form, before it is even asked by His disciples.

> *For the Lord himself shall descend from heaven with a shout with the voice of the archangel, and with the trump of God; and the dead in Christ shall rise first;*
> 1 Thessalonians 4:16

The Lord Jesus descends from heaven with a shout. More than likely, this means all the inhabitants of heaven shouting in unison. The archangel announces that "the bridegroom cometh." The trumpet of God sounds as the King of Kings appears. There are three distinct heavenly sounds in that verse.

> *⁹And, when he had spoken these things, while they beheld, he was taken up, and a cloud received him out of their sight. ¹⁰And while they looked up*

steadfastly toward heaven as he went up, behold, two men stood by them in white apparel. [11] Who also said, Ye men of Galilee, why stand ye gazing up into heaven? This same Jesus who is taken up from you into heaven, shall so come in like manner as you have seen him go into heaven.

Acts 1:9-11

It is interesting to note that Jesus was taken up out of their sight (not a split-second) because they continued to gaze at this super-natural phenomenon. The angels also said that He would return in like manner—again, not in a split-second.

The eyewitnesses beheld Him going until a cloud, which blocked Him from their view. It should be correct to believe that we shall see Him when He returns, just as they saw Him when He left. The angels did say in verse 11, "...Shall [he] so come in like manner as you have seen him go into heaven" (brackets added).

Let's put all the scriptures together and see a better-rounded itinerary of the rapture process in its proper sequence:

1. The Lord Jesus descends from heaven with a shout.
2. The archangel announces, "The bridegroom cometh. Go ye out to meet him."
3. The trumpet of God sounds as the King of Kings appears.
4. The Lord Jesus sends His angels to the four winds to gather His elect.
5. The dead in Christ rise first (resurrected).
6. We who are alive and remain are instantly changed (transfigured) in the twinkling of an eye; we are changed from mortality to immortality.

7. The five foolish virgins (Christians) light up, but their immortal glow goes out and they ask the five wise virgins (Christians) to share their oil (Holy Spirit) with them.
8. The wise tell them that the oil (Holy Spirit) is not something that can be shared, but must be received on an individual basis.
9. The five foolish virgins (Christians) go out and attempt to fix the lack of oil (Holy Spirit) issue.
10. While the five foolish virgins (Christians) are attempting to fix the lack of oil (Holy Spirit) issue, the five wise virgins (Christians) are taken up to meet the Lord Jesus in the air.

How long will the rapture process take? That is a good question that we don't have a specific answer for. The Bible does not clearly say. However, Jesus does use the word *hour* when referring to it. The word *hour*, as used in the Bible, could be referring to a portion of an hour. That could be anything from a few minutes to the better part of an hour.

We need to understand that there is a process underway in the rapture event and not a split-second disappearance. Another detail that should grab our attention is that God is not the author of confusion.

> *For God is not the author of confusion but of peace,*
> *as in all churches of the saints.*
>
> 1 Corinthians 14:33

Planes, trains, buses, and cars crashing sound like a lot of confusion. We can safely assume that this deception came from Satan, our enemy and the Father of Deception. Our Heavenly Father does things decently and in order.

> *Let all things be done decently and in order.*
>
> 1 Corinthians 14:40.

Chapter Four

The Transfiguration
(A Glimpse of the Rapture Process)

¹And after six days Jesus taketh Peter, James and John, his brother, and bringeth them up into a high mountain apart. ²And was transfigured before them; and his face did shine like the sun, and his raiment was as white as the light. ³And, behold, there appeared unto them Moses and Elijah talking with him. ⁴Then answered Peter, and said unto Jesus, Lord, it is good for us to be here; if thou wilt let us make here three tabernacles (booths), one for thee, and one for Moses, and one for Elijah. ⁵While he yet spoke, behold, a bright cloud overshadowed them, and, behold, a voice out of the cloud, which said, This is my beloved Son, in whom I am well pleased; hear ye him. ⁶And when the disciples heard it, they fell on their face, and were sore (very much) afraid.

Matthew 17:1-6

The author of the Bible, the Holy Spirit, uses a lot of symbolism and numerical significance when portraying Bible stories.

The transfiguration of Christ is a good example of this. Let's take notice of how this story begins: "After six days Jesus taketh." The symbolism representing the rapture starts right away. Six is the numerical equivalent of mankind, because mankind was created on the sixth and final day of God's creation, as we have already discussed. Now, let us also notice that Jesus is taking something as it relates to mankind.

Perhaps we should address all the symbolism that is contained in the transfiguration account and what it represents. The disciples that Jesus did not take with him represent people who think they are Christians but really are not. Peter, James, and John represent devoted Christians that fully believe they will be taken in the rapture. However, their lack of oil (Holy Spirit) prevents them from participating, even though they witness this supernatural event.

Jesus describes this group as foolish virgins (Christians) in Matthew 25:3:

> *They that were foolish took their lamps (salvation),*
> *and took no oil with them.*
>
> Matthew 25:3

Another interesting insight comes from Luke's account in Luke 9:32:

> *But Peter, and they that were with him, were heavy*
> *with sleep; and when they were awake, they saw his*
> *glory, and the two men that stood with him.*
>
> Luke 9:32

Christians who have accepted God's plan of salvation but are not yet filled with the Holy Spirit could be considered foolish and asleep. They will wake up in time to witness the rapture process but will not participate.

Moses represents the dead in Christ that will be raised and transfigured. Elijah represents we who are alive and remain that shall be transfigured in the twinkling of an eye. This group will not experience natural, physical death, just as Elijah did not experience natural, physical death. Christ represents Himself, and the whole process culminates with both groups meeting the Lord in a high place in the clouds. The voice from heaven represents the heavenly sounds which mark the beginning of the rapture process.

Many Bible scholars suggest that the transfiguration of Christ is a glimpse of His future kingdom beginning with His millennial, or thousand-year, reign on earth. Actually, the transfiguration is a glimpse of the rapture process, that is the first step in a chain of events, leading to His Millennial Reign on earth.

In the transfiguration account, Jesus demonstrates a change awaits the oil-filled (Holy Spirit–filled) Christians: faces shining like the sun and raiment as white as the light. This is what the angels that are sent to the four winds will be looking for.

Peter symbolizes the foolish virgins in Matthew 17:4 when he suggests building tabernacles, or booths, as he tries desperately to participate in this supernatural event. However, his natural, religious efforts are not to be substituted for the supernatural filling when God's Holy Spirit (oil) enters and begins working through a human vessel.

A common misconception about the transfiguration is that it was only a "vision" and not an actual supernatural event. Just because Jesus used the word vision (sight from God) in Matthew 17:9 doesn't mean the three disciples didn't see the transfiguration with their natural eyes. If Peter, James, and John did not see the transfiguration with their natural eyes, Jesus would not have taken them away by themselves. He could have left them with the other disciples that would not have had the vision.

Peter, James, and John saw into the spiritual realm with their natural eyes. This is something that rarely happens, so calling it a vision (viewing) into the spiritual realm would be appropriate.

Another point that should be emphasized is the three disciples fell asleep, and when they were awake, they witnessed the transfiguration of Christ. These disciples had all five natural senses operating.

> [16]*For we have now followed cunningly devised fables when we made known unto you the power and coming of our Lord Jesus Christ, but were eyewitnesses of his majesty.* [17]*For he received from God, the father, honor and glory, when there came such a voice to him from the excellent glory. This is my beloved Son, in whom I am well pleased.* [18]*And this voice, which came from heaven we heard, when we were with him in the holy mount.*
>
> 2 Peter 1:16-18

Peter describes himself as an eyewitness to this event and heard a voice from heaven. The transfiguration of Christ was a literal change that took place to His natural form and was visible to the natural eye. The three disciples were able to see and hear this supernatural event. They had a glimpse into the spiritual realm and a preview of the change that awaits oil-filled (Holy Spirit-filled) Christians as the rapture process begins.

Chapter Five

Parable of the Ten Virgins

Most Christians believe that when our Lord Jesus returns, He will be taking all committed Christians home to be with him. A popular belief about the parable of the ten virgins is that five are committed Christians, and five think they are Christians, but do not demonstrate a relationship with Christ.

Is this really what Jesus is saying to us in this parable? He clearly identifies what group shall be taken and what group shall be left behind. It is very important that we understand what He is saying in this parable, because the truth in His words will affect each one of us individually. That truth will be the determining factor in whether we participate in the rapture or are left behind, so let's pay very close attention!

> *¹Then shall the kingdom of heaven be likened unto ten virgins, who took their lamps and went forth to meet the bridegroom. ²And five of them were wise, and five were foolish. ³They that were foolish took their lamps, and took no oil with them. ⁴But the wise took oil in their vessels with their lamps. ⁵While the bridegroom tarried, they all slumbered*

and slept. ⁶And at midnight there was a cry made, Behold, the bridegroom cometh; go ye out to meet him. ⁷Then all those virgins arose and trimmed their lamps. ⁸And the foolish said unto the wise, Give us of you oil; for our lamps are gone out. ⁹But the wise answered, saying, Not so, lest there be not enough for us and you; but go rather to them that sell, and buy for yourselves. ¹⁰And while they went to buy, the bridegroom came, and they that were ready went in with him to the marriage; and the door was shut. ¹¹Afterward came also the other virgins saying, Lord, Lord, open to us. ¹²But he answered and said, Verily I say unto you, I know you not. ¹³Watch, therefore, for ye know neither the day nor the hour in which the son of man cometh.

Matthew 25:1-13

The first thing that we should notice is what group of people He is talking about in this parable. In verse 1, He uses the phrase "kingdom of heaven"—not kingdoms of earth. He clearly is telling a parable about Christians (His children)—believers who demonstrate a relationship with Him. Some might say we are all God's children, but that would be an incorrect statement. The truth is, that we are all God's *creation*. We don't become children of God until we accept and personalize salvation, which He provides through Christ's redemptive work.

Once a believer accepts and personalizes God's plan of salvation through Christ, they become citizens of heaven. Although our location does not change physically, our citizenship, in a spiritual sense, does. We become God's vessels on earth that He can use to accomplish His will. You might say we are heaven's ambassadors on earth. The Holy Spirit (oil) is the empowerment that God has given to us as ambassadors to fulfill His will.

But ye shall receive power, after the Holy Spirit is
come upon you; and ye shall be witnesses unto me
both in Jerusalem, and in all Judea, and in Samaria,
and unto the uttermost part of the earth.

Acts 1:8

The level or degree to which we are filled with the Holy Spirit
is left entirely up to us. You might say it is a personal decision and
quest that determines the degree or amount that we are filled. God
does not determine this filling and empowerment. Each individual
Christian ambassador has equal access to Holy Spirit empowerment.

[18]And be not drunk with wine, in which is excess, but
be filled with the Spirit. [19]Speaking to yourselves in
psalms and hymns and spiritual songs, singing and
making melody in your heart to the Lord.

Ephesians 5:18, 19

Those people who do not accept and personalize God's plan
of salvation through Christ continue to be citizens of earth, not
heaven, and do not have access to the Holy Spirit's (oil's) filling
and empowerment.

So Jesus is clearly talking about citizens of heaven, not earth,
in Matthew 25:1. He continues in this same verse with the descrip-
tive term virgins (Christians). Both of these descriptions are used
in His opening statement of this parable, "kingdom of heaven" and
"virgins" (Christians).

In verse 2, our Lord separates the group of ten virgins (Christians)
into two groups: five wise and five foolish. Notice that he doesn't
say five were wise and five were ignorant. A statement like that
would indicate five Christians and five non-Christians. The difference between "ignorant" and "foolish" is quite interesting.

Webster's dictionary defines "ignorant" as "having no knowl-
edge or understanding of a certain thing." This would go on to

describe non-Christians, or citizens of earth. Contrarily, Webster's also defines "foolish" as "lacking in good sense or judgment." This would be describing Christians that do not use all that is available to them, even though they are citizens of heaven.

Many non-Christians believe in God. They might even believe that Christ died for the sins of all mankind. They may even believe that they are Christians because they believe in God and attend church regularly. Belief in God and church attendance does not produce salvation (new birth).

Non-Christians are ignorant of the new birth (salvation) and what happens when a believer personally receives Christ's atonement into their own life. Because they have not personalized this truth, they are not yet citizens of heaven.

Our Lord uses the word *foolish* in Matthew 25:2 because these virgins (Christians) were not using all that is available to them. They believe they have the Holy Spirit but are not actively using the gifts (tools) that He provides. Any virgin (Christian) that does not use the gifts that are available because they have no need for them would be lacking in good sense of judgment, or "foolish."

We find in the Matthew 25 parable, in verses 3 and 4, that Jesus continues to separate the two groups of virgins. The foolish virgins are taking their lamps, representing salvation, without extra oil because they think they have enough. They were taught that upon receiving salvation, the Holy Spirit was automatically received.

The wise virgins made sure they had enough oil (Holy Spirit) with them for their lamps. These Christians were taught that the filling of the Holy Spirit was not automatic at the time of salvation. The filling of the Holy Spirit is something that must be asked for and sought after. When this filling occurs, there will be signs and evidence that defy natural explanation.

In Matthew 25:7-8, it is interesting to note that all ten virgins (Christians) arose to the rapture cry. They all thought they would be meeting the Lord in the air. All ten lamps were lit initially! People that think they are Christians but really are not will not be lighting up at all. Only citizens of heaven will be lighting up, or "transfigured."

As mentioned in the parable, the five foolish virgins (Christians) who thought they had enough oil realize they do not when their lamps go out (the transfiguration glow goes out). Then the foolish virgins are trying to borrow some oil (Holy Spirit) from the wise. That, however, is not something that can be borrowed. It is a personal decision we all must make as citizens of heaven. We can receive the Holy Spirit and use the gifts which He provides, or decide we don't need them in our Christian walk.

Every believer that has experienced salvation must ask to receive the Holy Spirit individually.

> *If ye then, being evil, know how to give good gifts unto your children: how much more shall your heavenly Father give the Holy Spirit to them that ask him?*
> Luke 11:13

Only believers who have received salvation are in a position to ask. People who think they are Christians but really aren't are in no position to receive any oil (Holy Spirit.) Their vessels are not ready to receive because salvation has not yet occurred.

> *Neither do men put new wine into old bottles: else the bottle break, and the wine runneth out, and the bottles perish: but they put new wine into new bottles, and both are preserved.*
> Matthew 9:17

People who think they are Christians but really are not, will not be lighting up at all when the trumpet blows. If they do not light up, they will not be able to go out! Jesus is clearly talking about ten virgins (Christians) who all have the capacity to receive oil (Holy

Spirit.) All ten virgins have been made worthy receptacles of the Holy Spirit by the blood of the Lamb (Jesus).

The differences between the wise and the foolish virgins are very important. The root cause of this difference is what we have been taught concerning the receiving and filling of the Holy Spirit. More on this in the next chapter.

Suffice it to say, for now, that the degree to which we can be filled with the Holy Spirit is left entirely up to us. We can have a little oil or a lot of oil. We can light up and then go out, or we can light up and stay lit!

Let us notice one more thing about this parable in Matthew 25:11. In this verse, the foolish virgins are pleading with God to accept them and let them in. It is clear that these Christians thought they would be taken and are upset that they were not. Non-Christians and people who think they are Christians will be wondering what happened. They will not be debating with Jesus about being left behind. Their understanding of this event (rapture), or lack of it, does not allow them to desire participation. They will be seeking worldly answers from other non-Christians that were also left behind.

Another misconception in this parable is verse 12. In this verse, the Lord says to them, "I know you not." Some teachers have said that this group (foolish Christians) are really non-Christians because of His response to them. What the Lord means is that He doesn't know them on a spiritual (Holy Spirit) level. They have received salvation through Christ and believed they would be taken in the rapture. However, the filling of the Holy Spirit has not yet occurred in their lives. In many cases, it is because they were taught that both events happen at salvation. The Lord doesn't say they won't be going to heaven. He does say they will not be going to heaven by the rapture process.

The rapture process is reserved for blood-washed, born-again Christians that have received the filling of the Holy Spirit and use His gifts (tools that defy natural understanding), to glorify the name of Jesus. The rapture is the collection process the Creator uses to gather all of the oil (Holy Spirit) on earth that is contained in human vessels. The foolish virgins do not have enough oil to collect because their transfiguration glow went out. They had enough oil to light up, but did not have enough oil (Holy Spirit) to stay lit.

Chapter Six

The Oil Question

There is a lot of confusion in the ranks of Christianity today. Denominational and non-denominational churches have different views concerning a wide variety of spiritual topics. This subject will be no different.

How much oil (Holy Spirit) is enough to keep our lamps from going out when our Lord Jesus appears? The answer to that question will be the deciding factor for each one of us and will determine whether we are taken or whether we are left behind.

First of all, let's start with a teaching that currently exists in the body of Christ.

> *Then Peter said unto them, "Repent and be baptized, every one of you in the name of Jesus Christ for the remission of sins, and ye shall receive the gift of the Holy Ghost.*

Acts 2:38

Many Christians believe that the Holy Spirit is automatically received at the time of their conversion (new birth). Many pastors teach this doctrine based on Acts 2:38. Just because the Holy

Spirit leads us to the place of repentance in Christ doesn't mean we are automatically filled. Another way to say this would be that the oil (Holy Spirit) is not automatically poured into our vessels at the point of conversion. The foolish virgins (Christians) will not be realizing this truth until it is too late. What a sad day that will be for them!

Let's look at some more scriptures where Peter is addressing the subject of receiving the Holy Spirit.

> *[14] Now when the apostles which were at Jerusalem heard that Samaria had received the word of God, they sent unto them Peter and John: [15] Who, when they were come down, prayed for them, that they might receive the Holy Ghost: [16] (For as yet he was fallen upon none of them: only they were baptized in the name of the Lord Jesus). [17] Then laid they their hands on them, and they received the Holy Ghost.*
>
> Acts 8:14-17

It is interesting to note that Peter did not repeat what he said in Acts 2:38. If receiving the Holy Spirit was automatic upon receiving Christ for the remission of sins, he would have said that. Maybe Peter should have said something along the lines of: "Because you have received Christ and been baptized, you shall receive the Holy Spirit." "There is no need for us to pray for you, or do not worry about it, because it is already done." Statements like these would be consistent with what Peter said in Acts 2:38, according to the doctrine which teaches salvation and receiving the Holy Spirit happen together.

Many Christians who accept this doctrine also believe they have received the Holy Spirit because the fruits of the Spirit are evident in their lives.

> *But the fruit of the Spirit is love, joy, peace, long-suffering, gentleness, goodness, faith, [23] meekness, temperance: against such there is no law.*
>
> Galatians 5:22-23

One would have to agree that the fruit of the Spirit needs to be evident in every Christian's life. If that, however, is the only evidence that the Holy Spirit has been received, there may be a problem. People of the world that have not yet received salvation can also demonstrate many of these fruits without the Holy Spirit. Some very important, influential, and benevolent people display these fruits through charity, teaching, and self-sacrifice, yet the new birth in Christ has not yet happened in their lives.

If we are trying to prove that a supernatural God in the form of the Holy Spirit has taken up residence in us, should there not be supernatural evidence that proves that fact? By supernatural, we mean evidence that cannot be duplicated through natural methods or means. Perhaps we should let the Lord Jesus give us some valuable insights when it comes to receiving the Holy Spirit.

> *But ye shall receive power, after that the Holy Ghost is come upon you: and ye shall be witnesses unto me both in Jerusalem, and in all Judea, and in Samaria, and unto the uttermost part of the earth.*
>
> Acts 1:8

The Lord Jesus gave these final instructions just prior to His ascension. The Greek word He uses for *power* is *dynamis*, as Strong's Concordance states, meaning "power, ability, miracle, mighty works." This is the same Greek word that we derive our word "dynamite" from. The Lord continues to clarify what He means in another part of His final instructions.

¹⁵ And he said unto them, "Go ye into all the world, and preach the gospel to every creature. ¹⁶ He that believeth and is baptized shall be saved; but he that believeth not shall be damned. ¹⁷ And these signs shall follow them that believe; In my name shall they cast out devils; they shall speak with new tongues; ¹⁸ They shall take up serpents; and if they drink any deadly thing, it shall not hurt them; they shall lay hands on the sick, and they shall recover.

Mark 16:15-18

In modern Christianity, this portion of Scripture is referred to as the "Great Commission." There are some that might ask at this point, "What does evangelizing the world and the individual filling of the Holy Spirit have to do with each other?"

Actually, the answer to that question would be *everything*.

The world is covered with multitudes of religions, all trying to promote their own beliefs. The difference between all those religions and Christianity is threefold.

1.   Only Christianity has Christ.
2.   Only the saved can receive Holy Spirit empowerment.
3.   Only Christians who have received Holy Spirit empowerment can demonstrate this fact through supernatural evidence that cannot be obtained through natural methods or means.

Christ clearly describes this truth in the Great Commission. Countless times throughout the Bible, the written truth is twofold:

1.   There is the initial truth, obtained by reading and understanding.
2.   There is deeper truth, obtained by digging and meditating.

The deeper truth does not negate the initial truth, but rather adds a wider scope of what is being presented. Verse 17 in the Great Commission is a good example of this.

> *And these signs shall follow them that believe; In my name shall they cast out devils; they shall speak with new tongues;*
>
> Mark 16:17

When this verse was translated from Greek into English, the Bible translators added punctuation where they thought it should go.

When modern punctuation is removed, it has a different implication:

> *And these signs shall follow them that believe In my name shall they cast out devils they shall speak with new tongues*
>
> Mark 16:17

The Lord Jesus spoke these words concerning those who believe in His name. Many names have been attributed to the Lord Jesus in the New Testament. The name we are going to focus on here is found in Matthew 1:23:

> *Behold, the virgin shall be with child, and shall bring forth a son, and they shall call his name Immanuel, which, being interpreted, is God with us.*
>
> Matthew 1:23

The name *Immanuel* is more of a characterizing description than a title. It literally means "God with us." Since the day of Pentecost, when the Holy Spirit was poured out on the 120 disciples, God has been with us through His Holy Spirit. He literally dwells in the temple of our bodies.

We can use this truth found in Mark 16:17 to realize what the Lord Jesus is really saying to us.

1. And these signs shall follow those who believe in My name.
2. And these signs shall follow those who believe in Immanuel.
3. And these signs shall follow those who believe God is with us.
4. And these signs shall follow those who believe they have the Holy Spirit.
5. And these signs shall follow those who believe the Holy Spirit resides in them.

The Lord Jesus is clearly saying that a supernatural occurrence of the Holy Spirit residing in us is going to be demonstrated by supernatural evidence. As Christians, we need to remember that we are citizens (ambassadors) of a heavenly kingdom and disciples (students) of the Lord Jesus. This fact needs to be demonstrated through the signs our Lord describes.

This is what separates Christianity from all the other religions of the world.

> *And they went forth, and preached everywhere, the Lord working with them, and confirming the word with signs following. Amen.*
>
> Mark 16:20

Some Christians believe the signs described in Mark 16 were only used to get the church started. After the last apostle died, these signs were no longer needed. That is merely a foolish excuse by those Christians to explain why there is no supernatural evidence in their own lives. The Lord Jesus does not confirm the apostles; He confirms His Word with signs following.

All religions have some form of writings they follow when promoting their beliefs. Christianity is the only one that can demonstrate supernatural evidence, according to the Bible, to support their beliefs. If the Christians within Christianity would allow the power of the Holy Spirit, that is supposed to be in them, to be demonstrated (signs), evangelizing the world would happen quickly.

There are other Christians at this point that might say, "I have received Christ and been washed from my sins by His blood. I believe I have the Holy Spirit and don't need supernatural signs to prove it."

Let's allow James to address that point.

> [17]*Even so faith, if it hath not works, is dead, being alone.* [18]*Yea, a man may say Thou has faith, and I have works; show me thy faith without thy works, and I will show thee my faith by my works.*
>
> James 2:17-18

Perhaps we should apply the same analogy found in the writings of James to the Holy Spirit question. It should go something like this: "You show me you have the Holy Spirit without supernatural signs evident in your life, and I will show you I have the Holy Spirit because of the supernatural signs evident in my life."

That may be one of the key differences between wise Christians and foolish ones.

The Lord Jesus clearly commands us, "Go ye into all the world and preach the gospel to every creature," as His opening instruction of The Great Commission (Mark 16:15). He continues by informing us in verses 17 and 18 of the signs (supernatural evidence) that will be needed to accomplish this global task.

"Supernatural Evidence"

1. Casting out demons (power of the spoken word)
2. Speaking with new tongues (edification and instruction)
3. Taking up serpents (protection)

4. If drinking deadly things (protection)
5. Laying hands on the sick (power of impartation)

Because this chapter's objective is to answer the oil question of how much oil is enough to keep our lamps from going out when the Lord Jesus appears, we will start with the initial supernatural evidence that was demonstrated when the "age" of the Holy Spirit began.

> *¹And when the day of Pentecost was fully come, they were all with one accord in one place. ²And suddenly there came a sound from heaven like a rushing mighty wind, and it filled all the house where they were sitting. ³And there appeared unto them cloven tongues as of fire, and it sat upon each of them. ⁴And they were all filled with the Holy Spirit, and began to speak with other tongues, as the Spirit gave them utterance.*
>
> Acts 2:1-4

Now we come to that very controversial and commonly misunderstood sign (supernatural evidence), speaking in tongues.

Here is a question that many will have: "Are you saying if I don't speak in tongues, I won't be taken in the rapture?" That is not what is being said. If you don't speak in tongues, it's because you haven't received the filling (baptism) of the Holy Spirit yet. (Not being filled [indwelt] by the Holy Spirit [oil] is the reason your lamp will go out, and you will be left behind.)

Speaking in tongues (our individual prayer language) is a by-product that occurs when a supernatural God, in the form of the Holy Spirit, dwells within our vessels. This union allows our spirit to pray using our voice, while bypassing our natural mind, as we are led by the Holy Spirit.

41

This intimate communication with our Heavenly Father could be called our "hotline to God." Another way to describe this prayer language would be to say that it's a one-on-one communication between our spirit and our Heavenly Father, and no one else is included—not even our natural mind.

Here are a few other common misconceptions about the indwelling presence of the Holy Spirit with the "initial" supernatural evidence of speaking in a language we've never learned.

1. Speaking in tongues is not needed.
2. Speaking in tongues is not for everyone.
3. Speaking in tongues has been misused in church and causes confusion.
4. Speaking in tongues shall cease.

> *[14]For if I pray in an unknown tongue, my spirit prayeth, but my understanding is unfruitful. [15]What is it, then? I will pray with the spirit, and I will pray with the understanding also; I will sing with the spirit, and I will sing with the understanding also.*
> 1 Corinthians 14:14-15

In his first letter to the Corinthian Christians, Paul is addressing the individual and corporate use of tongues. By corporate, we mean the usage of tongues in the setting of a church assembly. We will only be looking at his instructions concerning the individual usage of tongues; here's the reason why:

We all have been given twenty-four hours a day and seven days per week. That totals 168 hours in a week. If we spend two hours on Sunday morning and two hours Wednesday night at church (a corporate setting), that would be only four hours out of 168 total hours per week. Mathematically speaking, that would be 2 percent of our weekly time. We are going to look at the 98 percent of our time per week not in a corporate setting and the usage of tongues in our individual communication with our Heavenly Father.

Another teaching point that Paul makes about our individual prayer life is found in 1 Corinthians 14:15.

1. Praying with our understanding
2. Singing with our understanding

These would be exercised in the language that we have been trained in—the same language we use for communicating with other people.

1. Praying in the spirit
2. Singing in the spirit

These would be exercised in a language we haven't been trained in—a language that our spirit knows but our mind doesn't. This would be a good example of supernatural evidence that defies natural understanding.

If we are only praying and singing with our understanding, we are only using 50 percent (half) of what is available to us. In any school, 50 percent is not a passing grade. Why not use 100 percent of the resources available to us by the Holy Spirit?

The Lord Jesus places even a stronger emphasis on this point. It's found in the Gospel of John.

> [23]*But the hour cometh, and now is, when the true worshipers shall worship the Father in "spirit" and in truth; for the Father seeketh such to worship him.* [24]*God is a spirit; and they that worship him "**must**" worship him in "spirit" and in truth.*
>
> John 4:23-24 (emphasis added)

Any Christian who prays and sings with their understanding yet feels they don't need to pray and sing in the spirit as well could be considered foolish. Remember the definition of foolish: "lacking in good sense or judgment."

Another point that Paul makes to the Corinthian Christians is that his desire is for them to ALL to speak with tongues.

> *I would that ye all spoke with tongues.*
>
> 1 Corinthians 14:5

The indications are quite clear that this supernatural evidence—of the indwelling presence of the Holy Spirit—is designed for everyone. The remainder of that verse describes the usage of tongues in Church. It should be safe to assume that if the individual Christian doesn't use tongues at home, they will not be doing so in a corporate setting.

The age of the Holy Spirit began on the day of Pentecost in the upper room with 120 disciples of the Lord Jesus. This age will continue until He returns to collect (rapture) vessels (Christians) that are containers of the Holy Spirit.

The Bible doesn't really say how much oil (Holy Spirit) is enough to keep our lamps from going out when Christ appears. That judgment will be left up to Him, the Collector. After all, He sent the Holy Spirit to begin with on the day of Pentecost, so it makes perfect sense that He will be the one to collect the Holy Spirit at the end of the age.

> *But when the Comforter is come, whom "I will send" unto you from the Father, even the Spirit of truth, who proceedeth from the Father, he shall testify of me.*
>
> John 15:26

One thing is for certain: we should all make sure that we are adding oil to our vessels daily. A better question at this point might be, "How do I add oil (Holy Spirit) to my vessel?"

There is only one way to receive the Holy Spirit and grow in His fullness: intimate, one-on-one communication with our Heavenly Father. There are two methods available for this intimate communication.

1. Prayer – with understanding and with the Spirit
   (praise)   (worship).
2. Word of God (Holy Bible) – study to show ourselves approved and not ashamed (2 Tim. 2:15).

Everything else we do for God is a by-product of these two methods.

As we lay aside our own personal affections and ambitions, we make more room in our vessels for oil (Holy Spirit). This adding, or filling, of the Holy Spirit is entirely up to us to decide. We determine individually how much space (time) is available for this to occur.

> *18And be not drunk with wine, in which is excess, but be filled with the spirit. 19Speaking to yourselves in psalms and hymns and spiritual songs, singing and making melody in your hearts to the Lord.*
> Ephesians 5:18-19

It is interesting that Paul compares being filled with the Spirit to being drunk with wine (verse 18). You don't get drunk with wine by drinking one glass. The process of getting drunk would be: glass after glass after glass—so is the filling of the Holy Spirit, yielding to Him: time after time after time. Actually, a better translation in verse 18 of "be filled" would be "be being filled."

Conclusion

The purpose of this book has been to clear up some rapture misconceptions and to open our eyes to a potential lack of the Holy Spirit's presence in our lives. This will be the determining factor of whether we are considered wise or foolish.

There is a vast supply of books written on receiving the Holy Spirit and the gifts that are available once that has occurred. It is every Christian's individual responsibility to make sure there is enough oil in their vessels by adding daily. Hopefully this book has drawn our attention to that very important truth.

Let's remember the Lord Jesus sent the Holy Spirit on the day of Pentecost. He fully expects us to use all that is available to reach the lost and make a positive Christian impact on their lives. Most of us are not going into the entire world to preach. Our world consists of where we currently are and what we're doing to influence that world for Christ.

As we start putting faithful action to the Word of God, the Lord Jesus will confirm that Word with signs (supernatural evidence) following.

CPSIA information can be obtained
at www.ICGtesting.com
Printed in the USA
FFHW021147130219
50534906-55811FF